IMAGES
of America

THE EVERGLADES

IMAGES
of America

THE EVERGLADES

Robert S. Carr and
Timothy A. Harrington

ARCADIA
PUBLISHING

Published by Arcadia Publishing
Charleston, South Carolina

Library of Congress Control Number: 2011937409

For all general information, please contact Arcadia Publishing:
Telephone 843-853-2070
Fax 843-853-0044
E-mail sales@arcadiapublishing.com
For customer service and orders:
Toll-Free 1-888-313-2665

Visit us on the Internet at www.arcadiapublishing.com

CONTENTS

ACKNOWLEDGMENTS

The authors would like to thank members of the staff of Everglades National Park for their assistance and access to the park's photographic archives: archivist Bonnie Ciolino was particularly helpful, and Melissa Memory provided important facts. The good staff at HistoryMiami—particularly Patricia Baranahoa, Dawn Hughes, and Becky Smith—was especially helpful. Neal Adam Watson of Florida Photographic Archives and Dennise Cunningham and Helen Landers of the Broward County Historic Commission provided welcome access to their images. Help from historian John Beriault and archivist Jim Clupper was especially valuable, and particular thanks go to Debbie Brownfield Carr for her relentless word processing. Special thanks go to Seth Bramson, who generously opened his vast archive and collection of South Florida history, to Patsy West, who identified many of our Seminole and Miccosukee images, and to Collins Forman, who contributed several images and important information.

INTRODUCTION

Florida's southern tip is America's plunge into the tropics. Nestled in south Florida's interior lies the Everglades, a shallow basin of sawgrass marshes interspersed with islands of pines and lush tropical hammocks. Cradled on the east by the Atlantic Coastal Ridge and on the west by cypress forests, the Everglades prior to modern development was three times larger than what is preserved within Everglades National Park and adjacent conservation areas.

Popular ideas of the Everglades celebrate its natural wonders as a sea of grass with a myriad of animals. Few realize that the Everglades also has a cultural landscape—a wetlands crisscrossed by Indian canoes for over 5,000 years. Home to small bands of Native American hunters and fisherman, the Everglades was the domain of the Tequesta and earlier Archaic Indians who created deep middens filled with artifacts and animal bones. These Native Americans paddled across the sawgrass prairie with ease, building thatched huts on the highest tree islands. Fish, turtles, snakes, and deer provided daily sustenance.

In the 16th century, the Spanish referred to the Everglades as Lago de Isletas ("lake of little islands"). At that time, the "Glades" stretched across the horizon—a low relief of sawgrass marsh studded with clumps of bay trees and occasional oak and cabbage palms. Ficus trees broke the horizon like lighthouse sentinels, providing landmarks and welcome evidence of dry lands below for travelers.

Exposure to European diseases resulted in the near extinction of the Tequesta by the mid-18th century. The finishing touches of their demise were inflicted by Creek and Yuchi raiding parties who ventured into the Glades seeking game and Indian slaves. By 1763, the Everglades was devoid of people. That changed with the arrival of the Seminoles in the early 19th century. Forced into southern Florida after the United States bought Florida from Spain, the Seminole built settlements clustered along the Atlantic Coastal Ridge on the eastern rim of the Everglades. The first two wars between the Seminoles and the US Army and the encroachment of pioneer settlements pushed the Seminoles onto remote Everglades islands and into the Big Cypress Swamp. In 1838, the security of their Everglades hideaway was shattered when Col. William Selby Harney led a daring expedition of soldiers and sailors into the region, its first penetration by nonnatives. The new battle tactic led to numerous military expeditions into the Glades, eventually forcing all but 300 Seminoles to reservations in Oklahoma.

After the Seminole Wars, new settlers arrived in southern Florida, leading to increased demand for land and an innovative idea: drain the Everglades and open millions of acres for farming. Six years after the end of the Second Seminole War, native Floridian and Harvard graduate Buckingham Smith conducted an assessment of the Everglades that would result in the reclamation of three million acres of wetlands.

Although dredging of the Caloosahatchee River was started in the 1880s by the industrialist Hamilton Disston, it was Napoleon Bonaparte Broward, elected governor of Florida in 1904, who made the drainage of the Everglades his campaign rallying cry and the mainstay for an economic boom in Florida. Five dredges began the work in Lake Okeechobee. The first dredge left Fort Lauderdale in 1906 digging the New River Canal northward and then joining it to the Miami Canal. The Miami Canal was completed in 1912. As the dredge broke through the higher elevations of the Atlantic Coastal Ridge, the waters of the Everglades poured into the Miami River, turning the clear water brown. Tens of thousands of acres began to dry as water tables fell. Fires broke out—some even burning the muck. Tree island communities expanded to what formerly had been wetlands. Drained areas of the northern Everglades were plowed into sugarcane fields.

Those settlers who lived on the lower reaches of the Everglades in Flamingo, Cape Sable, and Chokoloskee had their livelihoods threatened by unregulated commercial fishing and hunting (although many of these settlers were part of the illicit trade in plumes). Bird populations fell dramatically as rookeries were decimated in the hunt for plumes to decorate women's hats. Even alligators became scarce. The Audubon Society posted its first game warden, Guy Bradley, to the Everglades in 1904; he was killed by plume hunters in 1905. His death caused a national outrage and new laws that led to the end of plume hunting.

As drainage, development, overhunting, and overfishing diminished the diverse flora and fauna of the Everglades, the Florida's Federation Women's Clubs mobilized to save Royal Palm Hammock. From it, the first park of 2,090 acres was created in 1916, known as Women's Park; it eventually was renamed Royal Palm State Park and later donated to the federal government in 1929 to become the nucleus of a proposed national park and the location of its first interpretive center.

The movement to create a national park was a 30-year battle largely led by landscape architect Ernest Coe, who headed the Tropical Everglades National Park Association. His efforts and support from scientists like David Fairchild, John Kunkel Small, and Ales Hrdlicka helped educate politicians about the importance of its natural wonders. Marjory Stoneman Douglas authored *The Everglades: River of Grass*, creating a public awareness of this unique resource that helped set the stage for millions of visitors to experience Everglades National Park.

The grand opening of the park occurred on December 6, 1947, at the western gateway in Everglades City. Soon, millions of people would visit the park and experience a diverse array of environments from Florida Bay at Flamingo to Mahogany Hammock, Royal Palm Hammock, and the panoramic view of the sawgrass prairie at the Shark Valley Tower.

Despite the park's successful creation, there are constant threats and challenges from outside and inside the park. Freshwater flow from Lake Okeechobee is diverted for agricultural and urban use. A rising sea level brings saltwater intrusion from Florida Bay. Droughts often bring disastrous fires that can consume naturally protected tree islands. Exotic plants and animals, including an expanding population of pythons and boa constrictors, continue to outcompete native species. While the Tequesta left little more than the wake of their canoes, today's humans will need to balance environmental preservation with urban demands for water, farmlands, and new homes.

One

EVERGLADES SKIRMISHES

Over 500 years before the Seminoles arrived in South Florida, prehistoric Indians lived throughout the Everglades. Decimated by European diseases and eventually by Creek and Yuchi slave raids, the last of the Tequesta left for Cuba in 1763. These prehistoric potsherds were discovered around 1948 along Florida Bay by Audubon warden Charles Brookfield. (Courtesy of the Historical Museum of Southern Florida.)

Brev. Maj. Gen. Thomas Sidney Jessup was assigned to assume command of the Florida troops in 1836. Enforcing federal policy to remove all Indians from the Florida peninsula, Jessup initiated a system of interior and coastal forts to box the Seminoles into the Florida interior. His capture of Osceola under a flag of truce sparked a national controversy and debate. (Courtesy of the Broward County Historical Commission.)

The Seminole Wars sparked the first official interest in the Everglades that generated a number of surveys and maps. This was the first comprehensive map of the south Florida interior. It was published in 1856 by then Secretary of War Jefferson Davis, who later became the first president of the Confederate States. (Courtesy of the Historical Museum of Southern Florida.)

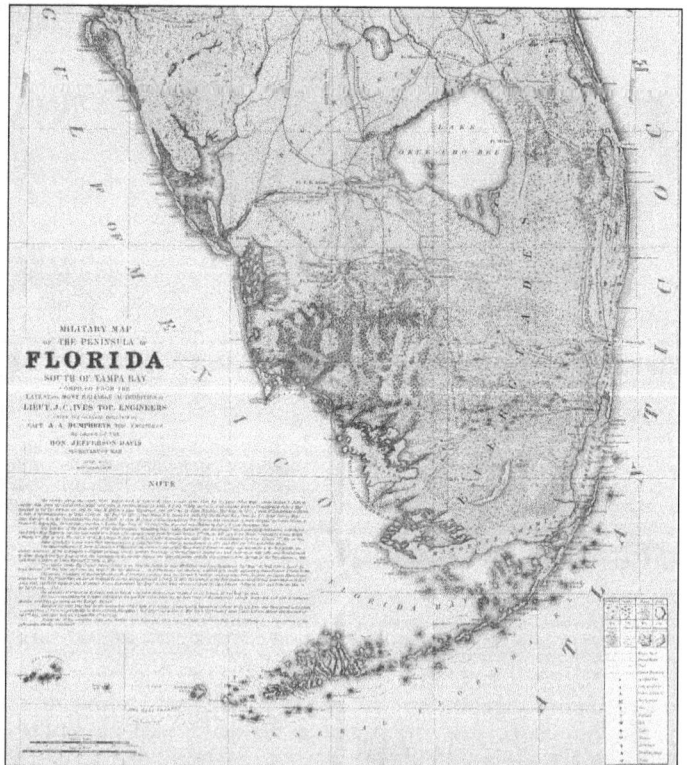

Gen. William Selby Harney was notorious as an "Indian fighter." His brash and fearless field command led US forces to their first foray into the Everglades. Using canoes, he pursued Chikika and his band of Spanish Indians, who had attacked and plundered the settlement at Indian Key. After killing Chikika and several warriors in a surprise raid, he hanged their bodies on an Everglades island known thereafter by the Indians as the Hanging Place. (Courtesy of the Library of Congress.)

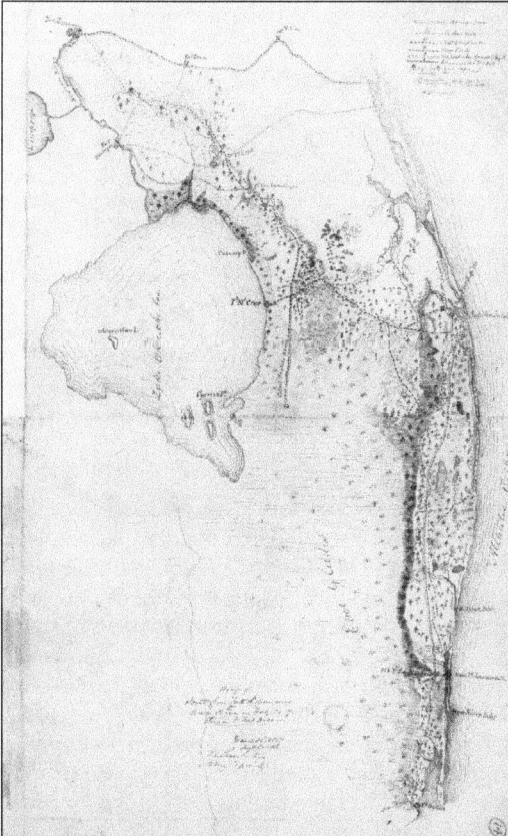

General Harney's tactics resulted in a successful penetration of the Everglades by US Army and Navy forces from their forts at Key Biscayne, Miami (Fort Dallas), and Fort Lauderdale. These expeditions resulted in two small, temporary forts being constructed in the Everglades—Fort Henry and Camp Wescott—both of which are protected archeological sites in Everglades National Park. (Courtesy of the Broward County Historical Commission.)

11

Col. Zachary Taylor received national attention and notoriety at the Battle of Lake Okeechobee. On Christmas Day in 1837, he and 800 regulars, along with 132 Missouri Volunteers, were lured into a killing zone of cut sawgrass by 400 Seminole warriors under the leadership of Alligator, Billy Bowlegs, and Chikika. Taylor's staggering losses of 26 dead and 112 wounded brought sharp condemnation from Sen. Thomas Hart of Missouri because of the disproportionate number of Missouri Volunteer casualties—including Col. Richard Gentry, founder of Columbia, Missouri. Taylor declared it a victory. It was the last conventional battle of the Seminole Wars; thereafter, the Indians used guerilla warfare. Promoted to general, Taylor exploited the battle in his climb to the 12th presidency of the United States. When Billy Bowlegs visited the White House in 1855 and saw a painting of Taylor on the wall, he was reported to have exclaimed, "Me whip him." (Courtesy of the Broward County Historical Commission.)

Billy Bowlegs was one of the principal chiefs during the Second and Third Seminole Wars. He gained prominence as a war chief after the capture of Osceola. Bowlegs evaded capture throughout the Second Seminole War, but after an interlude of peace while living in the Big Cypress, he was provoked into attacking an army patrol that crossed into his village and reportedly cut bananas from his fields. In 1858, Bowlegs was persuaded to surrender and immigrate to Indian Territory in Oklahoma. He arrived in New Orleans on his way to Arkansas with "two wives, five daughters, fifty slaves and one hundred thousand dollars cash"—his payment by the US government for immigrating with his band of 123 Seminoles. (Courtesy of the State Archives of Florida.)

After leading a patrol of 10 men and two wagons into the Big Cypress Swamp, 1st Lt. George Lucas Hartsuff was attacked by Billy Bowlegs and 40 warriors. Three soldiers were killed and scalped and their wagons burned. Seven soldiers, including four wounded, escaped back to Fort Myers. This attack provoked the Third Seminole War. (Courtesy of the Library of Congress.)

The Pine Islands, also known as Sam Jones Seven Islands, was one of the principal Seminole settlements in the Everglades. An attack by Col. James Bankhead in 1838 forced many of the Seminoles to abandon their camps and flee deeper into the interior, but they returned to the Pine Islands after the wars ended. Seminoles continued to live there until about 1910, when expanding white settlements forced them to abandon their villages. This is a photograph of a village in present-day Davie, taken in the 1890s by H.A. Ernst and published as a postcard. (Collection of Robert Carr.)

When the Third Seminole War ended, about 300 Seminoles remained scattered in small camps in the Everglades and the Big Cypress Swamp and near Lake Okeechobee. A photographer named Fields took this picture of a band of Seminoles with oxcarts camping in a pine flatwoods. (Collection of Robert Carr.)

Seminole adaptation to Everglades life relied on travel by dugout canoes, each manufactured from a single cypress tree. Seminoles propelled these canoes through the sawgrass with long wooden poles. (Collection of Robert Carr.)

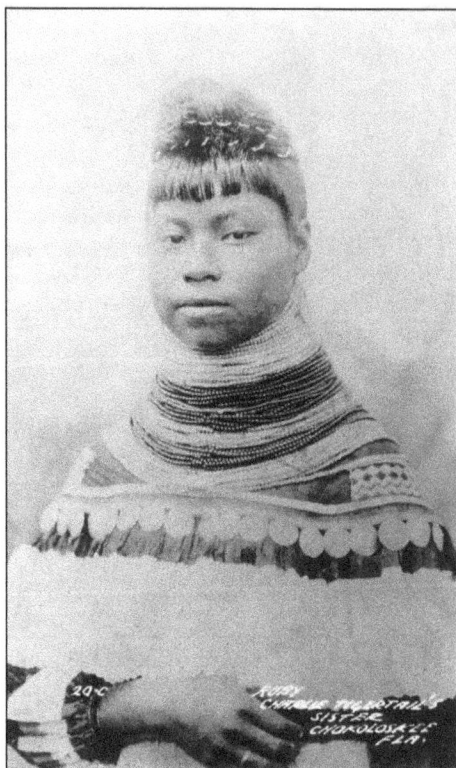

Ruby Tiger is of the Wind clan. This c. 1915 real-photo postcard shows her in traditional Seminole garb with a bodice, a large quantity of glass beads, and a coin necklace. A strand of beads was traditionally added each year, with the result that older Seminole women supported many pounds of beads. (Collection of Robert Carr.)

This postcard is of Billy Bowlegs III (Billy Fewell, known as Cofehapkee of the Black Snake clan), who was of no relation to the war chief with the same name. He reportedly had an African American father and a Seminole mother. Born in 1862, he was the grandson of Osceola through his maternal lineage. He became the first Seminole to be formally educated in English and was one of the first Seminoles to convert to Christianity. Billy died in 1965 and is buried in Ortona Cemetery near Moore Haven. (Collection of Robert Carr.)

Two

SEMINOLE AND MICCOSUKEE SURVIVAL

Seminoles are seen here unloading supplies at a store dock, possibly at Chokoloskee or Storter Store on the Barron River. (Courtesy of the Library of Congress.)

Seen in a c. 1909 photograph, Polly Parker (Ma-de-lo-yee, of the Little Bird clan), niece of Seminole War chief Billy Bowlegs, was reportedly born in 1826. She and her husband were forced to become guides for the US Army under Capt. Abner Doubleday during the Third Seminole War. After leading the army in circles, she was placed on a ship for immigration to Arkansas, from which she escaped at St. Marks and returned to south Florida. Parker lived out her life in a chickee west of Fort Pierce, where she died around 1940 at the age of 114 years. (Photograph by Harry E. Hill, Florida Photographic Concern [Fort Pierce], collection of Robert Carr.)

Tom Tiger was a Seminole leader in the late 19th century. Tiger is posing in front of a painted tropical backdrop in the company of a stuffed alligator around 1910. (Collection of Robert Carr.)

DESERTED SEMINOLE INDIAN VILLAGE   E

The booming development of coastal Miami and Fort Lauderdale forced hundreds of Seminoles to leave their villages on the eastern rim and resettle deeper in the Everglades or in commercial tourist camps. This real-photo postcard was taken about 1910 by a group of investors from Minneapolis traveling in southeast Florida to inspect real estate. This abandoned Seminole camp is likely one of the Snake Creek villages located near Miami. (Collection of Robert Carr.)

This postcard view of Seminoles posing in front of cars next to the Royal Palm Hotel in Miami was taken between 1906 and 1910. Seminoles were frequent visitors to Miami, where they traded pelts, plumes, and alligator hides for groceries, guns, and ammunition. (Photograph by Underwood, collection of Robert Carr.)

A 15528 Seminole Indians, Florida.

19

A Seminole guide takes an unknown tourist into a cabbage palm hammock to hunt around 1910. Meeting Indians was popular with tourists, who regarded the "unconquered" Seminoles as an exciting part of their Florida experience. (Real-photo postcard by Harry E. Hill, collection of Robert Carr.)

In this real-photo postcard, a Seminole woman prepares small game for a family meal. Seminoles subsisted on a variety of hunted, gathered, or farmed foods, including alligator, turtle, deer, coontie, pumpkin, and corn. Over time, they increasingly relied on store-bought goods. (Collection of Robert Carr.)

Charlie Tigertail created the first Seminole trading post. He constructed this western-style store on an Everglades tree island. (Courtesy of Library of Congress.)

Seminoles became increasingly reliant on automobiles and trucks for transportation. Cars became important on the Tamiami Trail, where they grew to be the favored means of reaching Miami and Naples for shopping. Eventually, cars became common on the Brighton and the Big Cypress Reservations. (Collection of Robert Carr.)

Seen in this c. 1940 real-photo postcard, Chokoloskee Island is an ancient shell-mound complex created by prehistoric people as they excavated canals and mounds. The island was used by the military in the Third Seminole War and eventually attracted pioneer settlers such as the McKinneys, the Santinis, and the Smallwoods, who constructed a store there. (Published by L.L. Cook, collection of Robert Carr.)

Smallwood's Store was built in 1906 by Ted Smallwood. It was operated as a post office and trading post until 1982, when it became a museum. The site was listed in the National Register of Historic Places in 1972. In 2011, the road to the store was destroyed by a developer, effectively isolating it and cutting off visitor access and revenue until a court-ordered injunction reopened the road. (Real-photo postcard published by L.L. Cook, collection of Robert Carr.)

The Jumper family poses next to Smallwood's Trading Post about 1920. The real-photo postcard includes Little Charlie (left) and Tommie "Squirrel" (right) of the Bear clan. The store is located on Chokoloskee Island, once proposed to become part of Everglades National Park but left out in the final park creation to avoid displacing the pioneer settler families, some of whom had been there since 1875. (Published by Ted Smallwood, collection of Robert Carr.)

Seminoles frequented the store from the early 1900s to the 1970s to purchase utensils and food. In this 1950s real-photo postcard view, the original tin advertising signs are still in place. Like most waterfront buildings in the Everglades, the store was built on pilings to keep the floor well above high tide. (Published by Ted Smallwood, collection of Robert Carr.)

Deaconess Harriet Mary Bedell wanted the Seminoles and Miccosukees to have a market for their crafts without having to rely on living in tourist villages, which she thought offensive. She was born in Buffalo, New York, in 1875 and became an Episcopalian missionary. In 1932, she founded the Glades Cross Mission near Everglades City, where she spent the rest of her life helping the Seminole tribe. (Courtesy of the State Archives of Florida.)

Deaconess Bedell helped market Seminole and Miccosukee products by organizing their crafts industry to create a reliable cash income. She successfully lobbied legislators in Washington, DC, to prohibit the import of Japanese imitations of Seminole crafts. Bedell died in 1969 and, as of 2009, was named as a saint by the Episcopal Church and is honored each January 8. (Courtesy of the State Archives of Florida.)

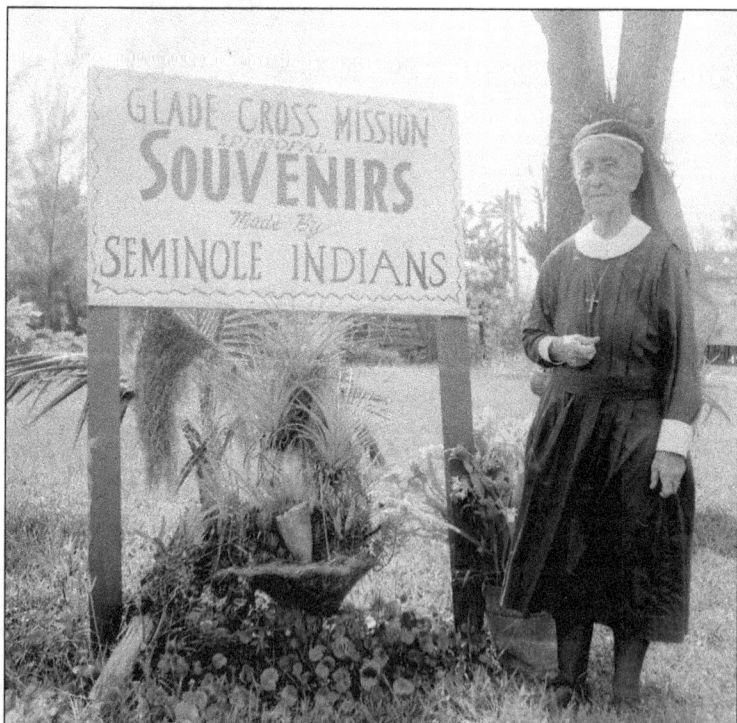

Seminoles developed crafts using local materials to create palmetto and pine-needle baskets, dolls, and other items. This real-photo postcard depicts Billie Tommie "Squirrel" Jumper (left) and her daughter Ruby Cypress (center), of the Bear clan, with Bedell-influenced baskets. (Collection of Robert Carr.)

Seminole independence was greatly advanced by tourist villages. The first village, created in 1917, was called Coppinger's Tropical Gardens on the Miami River and later became Pirate's Cove. By the 1920s, Musa Isle had become the most popular of the tourist villages. Both Pirate's Cove and Musa Isle stayed in business into the 1960s. Today, townhouses and a senior center have been built over the site. (Collection of Robert Carr.)

In this real-photo postcard, a Seminole hunter, brandishing a shotgun, wears a patchwork jacket, scarf, and floppy cowboy hat typical of men on the Brighton Reservation in the 1930s. (Postcard by Cook Inc., collection of Robert Carr.)

Three

THE GLADESMEN

"Uncle" Steve L. Roberts settled at Whitewater Bay in 1901 and then moved to Flamingo, opening its first hotel in 1915. Roberts and his descendants were associated with Flamingo until the creation of Everglades National Park in 1947. (Courtesy of the Historical Museum of Southern Florida.)

Gladesmen were otherwise uncategorizable, rugged individuals who subsisted in the wild—the backwoodsmen of the Everglades. One of them, Guy Bradley, went on his first plume hunt at seven years of age. The wholesale slaughter of wading birds for feathers for ladies' hats, however, got to his conscience; at age 32, he took a job with the Audubon Society as the Everglade's first game warden. (Courtesy of the National Park Service, Everglades National Park.)

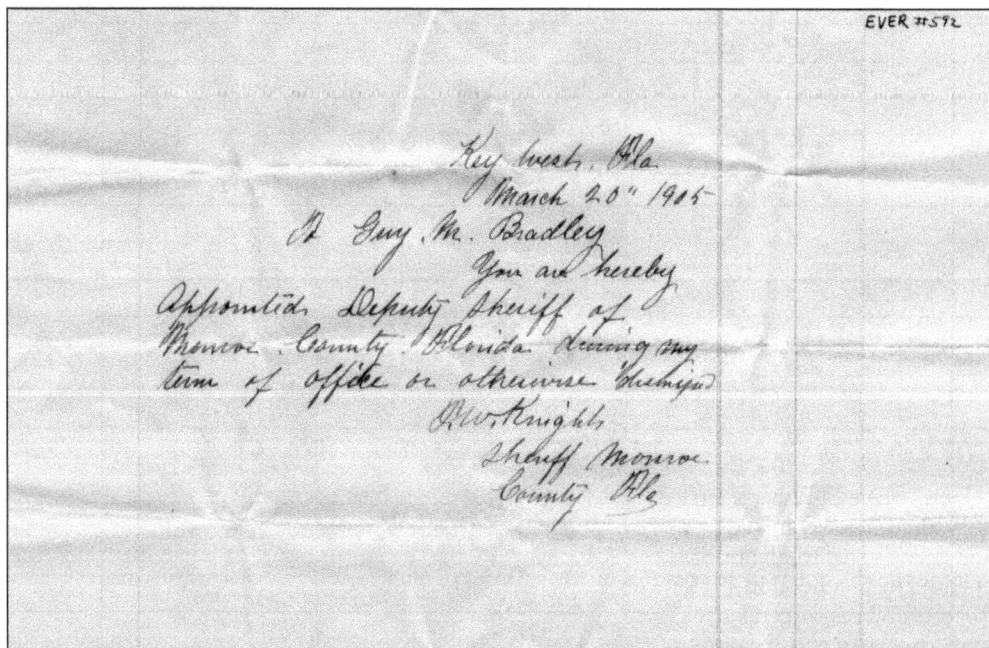

In 1905, with his reputation established, Bradley became deputy sheriff of Monroe County on the authority of this handwritten appointment. Bradley served at his post for three years, faithfully protecting bird rookeries throughout the Glades. (Courtesy of the National Park Service, Everglades National Park.)

In July 1905, Guy Bradley was killed near his home in Flamingo by former friend and fellow gladesman Walter Smith. Smith, a sharpshooter who had lost an eye for the Confederacy at the Battle of the Wilderness, shot Bradley as he was about to arrest Smith's teenage son for the third time for shooting birds in a rookery. Bradley's body was buried on a lonely beach at Cape Sable. (Courtesy of the Historical Museum of Southern Florida.)

The Bradley grave is visited by Audubon warden Charles Brookfield around 1948. Brookfield's book *They All Called it Tropical* recounts the life and death of Guy Bradley, the first martyr to the cause of conservation in the Everglades. (Courtesy of the Historical Museum of Southern Florida.)

Pictured is gladesman Randall Henderson. His brothers Allen and William Henderson are better known, being among the earliest Dade County law officers killed in the line of duty. Deputized into a posse formed to pursue the Rice Gang, which had just robbed the Bank of Homestead in 1916 (Dade County's first bank robbery), the brothers were shot in a gunfight. (Courtesy of the State Archives of Florida.)

Edgar J. Watson was a boisterous man with a checkered past who showed up in the Ten Thousand Islands in the southern Everglades and started a farm. He hired plenty of help, but his field hands tended to disappear ahead of payday, and some turned up dead. This is a real-photo postcard of his homestead on the Chatham River. Locals began to take Watson's boasts of having killed 57 men seriously. When he landed at Chokoloskee in the wake of the 1910 hurricane, he was met by a posse of 20 men and a hail of gunfire, killing him instantly. (Collection of Robert Carr.)

The African American seen at Smallwood's Trading Post in Chokoloskee in this c. 1920 real-photo postcard may be one of those who fired the fatal shot that ended the life of Edgar Watson. (Collection of Robert Carr.)

Unidentified gladesmen pose in front of their camp; a Glades skiff is tied to the bank. Hunting and fishing were a way of life. (Courtesy of the Historical Museum of Southern Florida.)

Tom Bryan and his brother Reed, teenagers at the time, came to the New River from north Florida with their father, Nathaniel, in the late 1800s to supervise work gangs building the Florida East Coast Railroad. Living off the land at first, Reed went into farming while Tom developed Fort Lauderdale's first electrical grid and telephone system. (Courtesy of the Historical Museum of Southern Florida.)

This real-photo postcard shows a group of hunters relaxing at "Camp Everglades"—an unknown location—between 1905 and 1910. Commercial hunting greatly diminished bird and alligator populations, eventually causing alligators to be placed on the endangered species list. (Collection of Robert Carr.)

Hunters on horseback bring in game to Bamboo Camp in January 1914. The camp, popular with hunters, is located in a pine island—likely the site of an earlier Seminole camp. The postcard is from a series published by expedition leader John Hachmeister. (Collection of Robert Carr.)

In January 1914, a chef sizes up game in the rather well-constructed living quarters of Bamboo Camp organized by hunter/entrepreneur John Hachmeister. Bamboo Camp was located in the Big Cypress Swamp, east of Naples. (Collection of Robert Carr.)

"Alligator Joe's" "Pals"

Other than as "Alligator Joe's Pals," these Glades hunters are unidentified. The man on the left has a lantern attached to his head for night hunting. The real Alligator Joe ran a tourist attraction of penned alligators in Palm Beach. (Collection of Robert Carr.)

Diamond Back Rattler

February - 1914

This real-photo postcard published by John Hachmeister of a diamondback rattlesnake killed in February 1914 was taken in front of the Naples Post Office. It was common practice for settlers and hunters to kill every snake they encountered. Fatal snakebites were rare, but at least one snakebite death, that of the son of Tom Alderman, occurred on Cape Sable in the early 1900s. (Collection of Robert Carr.)

Individualism was a given in the Everglades. Two unidentified gladesmen pose with a skiff and pole; the pole was adopted from the Seminoles. (Courtesy of the Historical Museum of Southern Florida.)

Three men in skiffs examine a wading bird. Shallow-draft skiffs, modeled after Seminole canoes, were the favored mode of transportation for gladesmen. (Courtesy of the Historical Museum of Southern Florida.)

An Everglades survey party pauses for a photograph in 1913. This image may depict the survey of Cape Sable conducted for the Model Land Company by the Biscayne Engineering Company. (Courtesy of the State Archives of Florida.)

A gladesman guides a boat through the Everglades in 1913. It was reported by Glen Simmons that one gladesman had poled 60 miles in one day. (Courtesy of the State Archives of Florida.)

This postcard reads, "In the Everglades. One of the men holding up two moccasin snakes that we have just killed. One of them was in a tree just over where we were having lunch. He died soon." (Postcard by R.W. Harrison [Key West], collection of Robert Carr.)

The main draw for fishermen in the southern Everglades was game fish such as tarpon and snook. This unidentified fisherman maintains his balance as he brings in the big one. (Courtesy of the Historical Museum of Southern Florida.)

A day's catch in the Everglades is captured here by Guy Phipps on the New River in Fort Lauderdale around 1912. Phipps recorded many of the features and daily life of the newly drained Everglades. (Collection of Robert Carr.)

A hunter tends to his lean-to, where the skins of his kill dry in the sun. Prices for feathers and skins varied, but in 1890 deer skins were 40¢ to 50¢ each, alligator skins were 10¢ a foot, and egret plumes $1 each. Within 10 years, egret feathers would be worth their weight in gold. (Courtesy of the Historical Museum of Southern Florida.)

Everglades fishermen clean their catch in the 1920s. Commercial fishing was an important livelihood throughout the Florida Bay settlements. (Courtesy of the State Archives of Florida.)

In this real-photo postcard, an airboat is being launched at Chokoloskee Island. Fishermen and hunters used the island trading post for selling pelts and skins. (Collection of Robert Carr.)

Moonshining was a popular but illicit activity in the Everglades. Moonshiners used remote tree islands to hide their enterprises. Al Capone is rumored to have maintained several stills in the Glades, including one on Loop Road. (Courtesy of the Historical Museum of Southern Florida.)

The man standing in a hand-hewn cypress dugout canoe in this c. 1943 photograph is thought to be Miccosukee Indian Charlie Cherry. He is standing in the canoe at a landing on an Everglades tree island. These dugouts were the models for the skiffs prized by gator hunters and commonly used by gladesmen. (Photograph by John Henry Davis, courtesy of the State Archives of Florida.)

Glades skiff builder Glen Simmons navigates his way through a sawgrass marsh near Florida City. His skiffs were inspired by the design of Seminole and Miccosukee dugouts. (Photograph by Robert L. Stone, courtesy of the State Archives of Florida.)

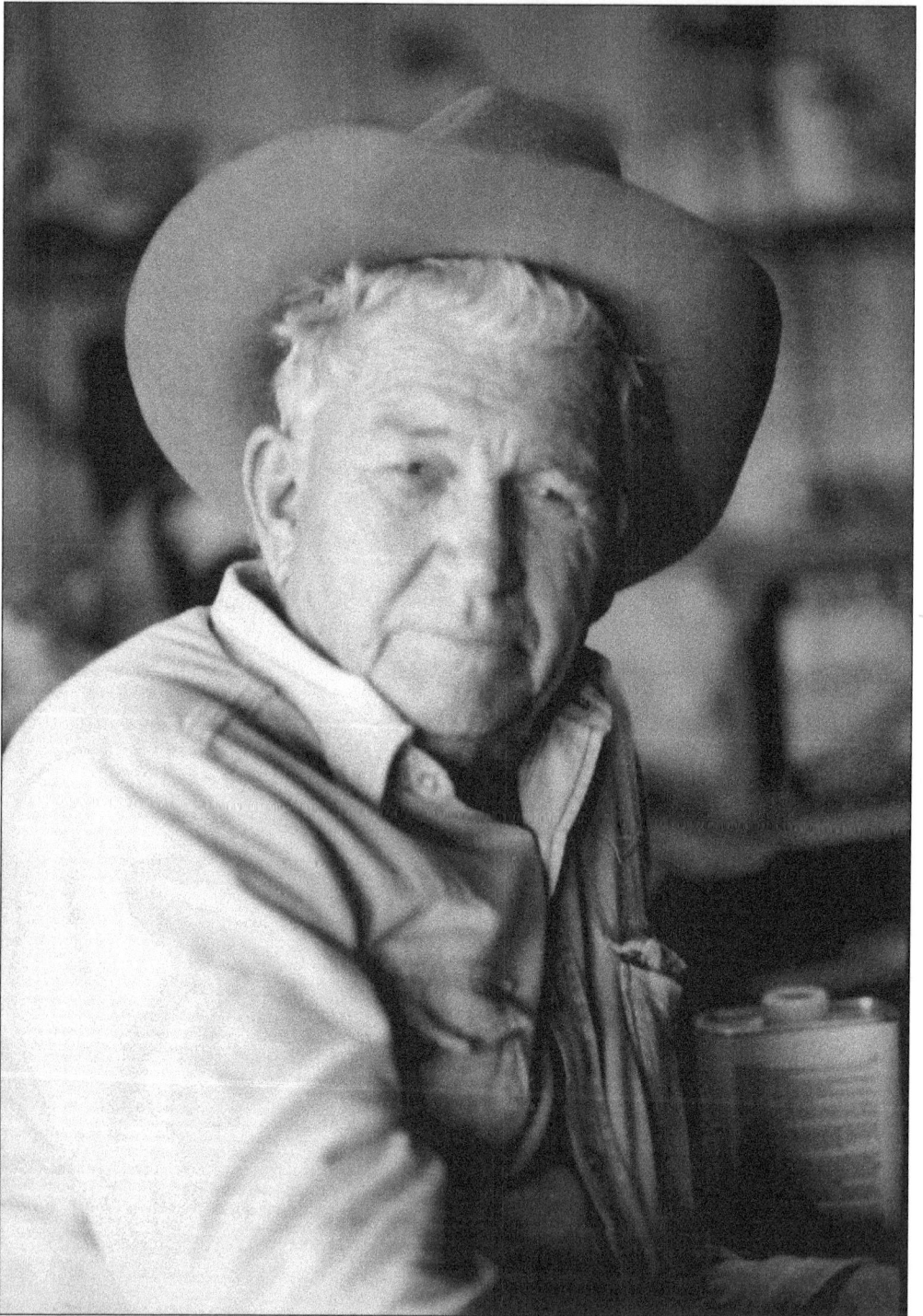

Gladesman Glen Simmons is seen in his workshop in Florida City. He was born in 1916 and began hunting and fishing in the Everglades in the 1920s. Simmons designed his own skiff especially adapted for the shallow waters of the glades. (Photograph by Robert L. Stone, courtesy of the State Archives of Florida.)

Four

DRAINING THE EVERGLADES

A dredge churns through a newly dug canal. The dredges *Okeechobee*, *Everglades*, and *Miami* operated in the Everglades between 1906 and 1909. It was estimated that Everglades muck was dredged at a cost of 13.1¢ per cubic yard for an overall operating cost of $306,000. (Courtesy of the State Archives of Florida.)

BUCKINGHAM SMITH

TABLET UNVEILING
April Third, Nineteen Hundred Forty-One

St. Augustine, Florida

BUCKINGHAM SMITH
SCHOLAR   DIPLOMAT
1810 – 1871

Pioneer Authority on Early Florida History
and Benefactor of St. Augustine's
Worthy Colored People

Buckingham Smith, a Harvard law graduate and scholar, had lived in Florida as a boy. He returned to Florida in 1848 when the US secretary of the treasury appointed him to assess the Everglades. He concluded his study by recommending that digging canals and deepening existing rivers and creeks could be used to reclaim the Everglades and to establish an agricultural economy in south Florida. In his report, Smith described the Everglades as "a place of profound and wild solitude . . . pervaded by silence." (Courtesy of the Florida Historical Society.)

In 1881, Hamilton Disston, a Philadelphia industrialist, bought four million acres of land from the State of Florida—land the federal government gave to the state under the Swamp Act of 1850—and set about developing it, fueling a land boom. His plan was to dredge the Kissimmee River floodplain and connect Lake Okeechobee with the Caloosahatchee River. One result was the successful cultivation of rice and sugarcane on reclaimed land. His Caloosahatchee River drainage program ultimately failed, as lands around the river became flooded because he had not dug southern and eastern canals from Lake Okeechobee. (Courtesy of the State Archives of Florida.)

William Sherman Jennings (a cousin of William Jennings Bryan) was elected Florida's 18th governor in 1900. Governor Jennings laid the groundwork for drainage and reclamation of the Everglades by settling claims and acquiring key pieces of land. In 1903 he wrote, "It will appear that the drainage of the Everglades is entirely feasible and practicable, thus reclaiming 3,760,000 acres, a large percentage of which would be feasible, and the most valuable agricultural land in the southern states." (Courtesy of the State Archives of Florida.)

Napoleon Bonaparte Broward followed his colleague Jennings to the governorship in 1905, largely propelled to office on his Everglades drainage platform. Carrying a map of the Glades everywhere, Governor Broward broadcast the message, "Water will run downhill!" His opponents countered, "You will drain the treasury before you drain the Everglades." Broward brought national attention to the project by inviting Theodore Roosevelt to inspect a drainage canal and winning the president's support. (Courtesy of the State Archives of Florida.)

Posing on a farm reclaimed from the Everglades, two populist Florida governors, William Sherman Jennings and his successor and collaborator Napoleon Bonaparte Broward (the architects, boosters, and enablers of Everglades drainage and reclamation), bask in their success. (Courtesy of the State Archives of Florida.)

Dredge men depended on surveyors to accurately plot the courses of canals and to lay out straight lines for the dredges to follow. Working at a disadvantage in the south Florida wilderness, surveyors often had to set their transits on wooden platforms raised above the soft, wet soil in order to keep their instruments level. (Courtesy of the State Archives of Florida.)

This c. 1904 political cartoon lampoons the gift of submerged federal lands to Florida. Uncle Sam is shown giving the Everglades to Miss Florida. "You may have these," he says, "if you drain and develop them." (Courtesy of the Historical Museum of Southern Florida.)

The dredging of south Florida began with the North New River Canal. On July 4, 1906, dredges began cutting through soil and limestone, angling sharply northeast to Lake Okeechobee from the south branch of the New River west of Fort Lauderdale. The spoil from dredging lined the riverbank in huge berms of sediment, which were exploited by squatters as sites for homes, stores, and, in one case, a post office. (Courtesy of the Broward County Historical Commission.)

The Miami Canal (right) flows south from Lake Okeechobee for 77 miles and into the Miami River. The dredge reached the headwaters of the Miami River in 1912. To join the river, and deepen it, the dredge smashed through the rocky ledge on the western side of the Atlantic Coastal Ridge and formed the Miami Rapids. An outrush of sediments polluted the clear waters of the river, and a brown torrent rushed into the ocean for days. (Collection of Robert Carr.)

This real-photo postcard depicts the construction of the dam (lock) on the North River Canal around 1910. The location, on the north side of present-day Interstate 595 in Plantation, is now a state historic site. (Postcard by Guy Phipps, collection of Robert Carr.)

All dredges were accompanied by quarter boats that brought supplies and men up the canals. This photograph shows a work barge loaded with wooden barrels. These barges carried food, fuel, and construction materials. (Courtesy of the State Archives of Florida.)

Governor Broward began the drainage project with two dredges, the *Everglades* and the *Okeechobee*, on the New River. From the North New River, the *Everglades* worked its way north to Lake Okeechobee; while from the South New River, the *Okeechobee* dug west to intersect the Miami Canal, which was headed south to join the Miami River. In this postcard, a dredge navigates the New River near the railroad trestle at present-day Las Olas Riverfront. (Collection of Robert Carr.)

The dredge bucket measured three feet across and could pick up a ton of sediment in a single scoop. (Courtesy of the National Park Service, Everglades National Park, EVER 17640.)

A group of tourists inspects the newly dredged New River Canal. The completion of the canal in 1912 unleashed a new wave of tourist excursions into the Everglades and stimulated travel between Fort Lauderdale and Lake Okeechobee. (Courtesy of the Broward County Historical Commission.)

The steamboat *Suwanee* is seen from two directions on the Caloosahatchee River in these photographs. A steamboat excursion along the beautiful Caloosahatchee River and Canal was a popular travel choice for tourists. The network of canals made cross-Florida excursions by boat between Fort Lauderdale and Fort Myers possible and comfortable. The *Suwanee* stopped at Ritta, Fort Lauderdale, and Miami. A round-trip ticket, including meals and a berth, cost $25. (Both, collection of Robert Carr.)

Five

FARMING THE EVERGLADES

The caption of this real-photo postcard reads, "Reclaimed Land in the Everglades' before being cleared—Florida Fruit Lands Company." (Collection of Robert Carr.)

Dredged canals drained the body of the Everglades, but ditches still had to be dug to drain farmland. This real-photo postcard depicts a mechanical ditcher digging at present-day Davie, near Fort Lauderdale, around 1906. Ditchers could dig a trench 4.5 feet wide at the top, 2 feet wide at the bottom, and 4.5 feet deep at the rate of 12 linear feet per minute. (Collection of Robert Carr.)

Seen in this real-photo postcard, the Buckeye Traction Ditcher, made in Findlay, Ohio, was used to excavate ditches across southeastern Florida from the New River Canal in Davie southward to Florida City. James B. Hill invented the steam-driven traction ditcher to drain northern Ohio's Old Black Swamp, the flood plain of Lake Erie, which was developed for farming after the Civil War. (Collection of Robert Carr.)

A Buckeye ditcher digs a drainage ditch on new farmland. After surveyors laid out the ditch, the ditcher was powered up and aligned and the digging wheel lowered. Dirt was carried to the top of the digging wheel, dumped from the bucket into a cross conveyor, and piled to one side of the ditch. Designed without spokes or an axle, the digging wheel could dig to a depth almost equal to its diameter. (Courtesy of the Broward County Historical Commission.)

In 1911, the Everglades extended eastward into present-day suburban Miami. This view of what is now suburban Kendall shows a pristine sawgrass prairie and a pine island. (Collection of Robert Carr.)

A group of investor/future farmers poses by a drainage ditch in the Everglades in 1910. The photographer sent this picture home to his niece in Kansas City. The postcard was postmarked in Miami on October 26, 1910. (Collection of Robert Carr.)

Starting for the Everglades.

This postcard depicts pioneer families as they start out on the trek from Fort Myers into the Everglades by oxcart. Settlers arrived in Immokalee and other parts of the Big Cypress Swamp as early as 1872. (Collection of Robert Carr.)

An oxcart crosses the prairie from Immokalee to the Big Cypress Swamp about 1915. The anonymous writer notes on the back of this real-photo postcard, "No habitations of any kind for the entire 18 miles but plenty cows." (Collection of Robert Carr.)

23   DR HOLMBERG ON BAYVIEW PARK PROPERTY

Dr. Holmberg inspects the Bayview Park property, still undrained, in this c. 1910 real-photo postcard. He was part of a large group of investors from Minneapolis who came by train to Miami to purchase Everglades lands. (Collection of Robert Carr.)

This real-photo postcard shows that the Weir & Pitts truck farm in Section 1 of Township 54 South, Range 40 East, was in the vicinity of Flagler Street, west of Northwest Fifty-seventh Avenue, in what is now urban Miami. (Collection of Robert Carr.)

The first roads into the Everglades, like the one in this real-photo postcard, were constructed of crushed limestone. Rock was quarried from the higher limestone ridge near the coast. (Collection of Robert Carr.)

In this real-photo postcard, oxen pull a wagon in the eastern Everglades. Roads improved access to newly cleared land and allowed homesteaders to bring farming supplies in and produce out by oxcart. (Collection of Robert Carr.)

Other forays into the Glades were braved in Model Ts. As seen in this real-photo postcard, potential landowners drove into the eastern Everglades in search of land, risking becoming bogged down in muck or stuck in holes. (Collection of Robert Carr.)

This Everglades sugarcane field was reportedly located in present-day Davie, likely near the South New River Canal. Davie, located just outside of Fort Lauderdale, became one of the first hubs of Everglades farming. (Courtesy of the Davie Historical Society.)

This is a bean field in the eastern Everglades in Broward County. Newly drained swampland provided thousands of acres of land for agriculture. The real-photo postcard was taken by Guy Philips around 1912. (Collection of Robert Carr.)

"There is but one Everglades" exclaims the mailer of this real-photo postcard, reporting on a shipment to market of a bumper crop of melons. (Published by Hunt and Akins [Fort Myers], collection of Robert Carr.)

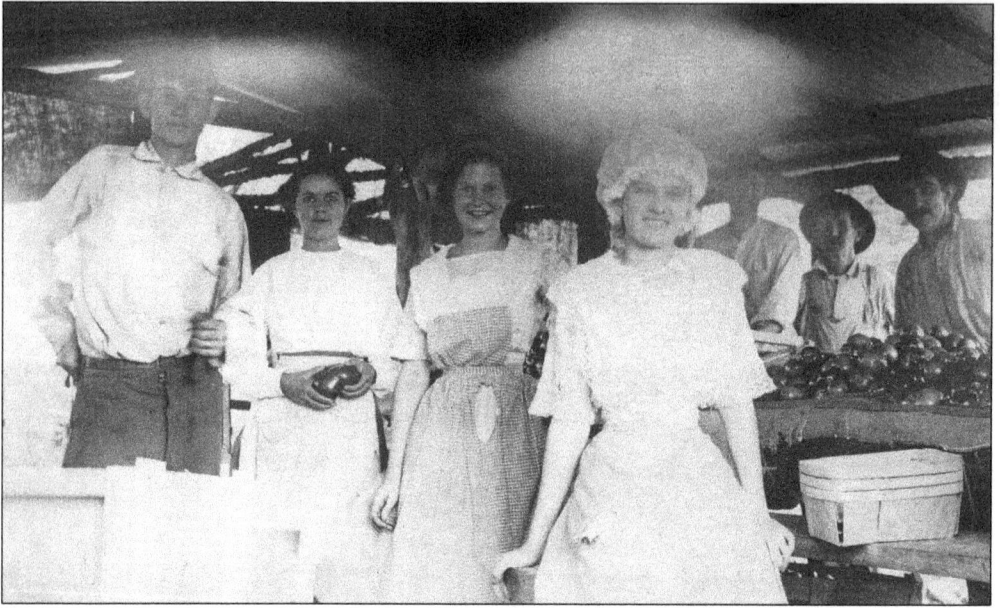

These young workers are in a tomato packinghouse in the eastern Everglades in Broward County. A booming economy, driven in part by investors and new farms, attracted thousands of settlers to south Florida, providing ample employment. (Courtesy of the Broward County Historical Commission.)

The Club House on the development of Security Farms Syndicate, about 23 miles west of West Palm Beach, fronting the Cross State Highway and Okeechobee Road Canal. 10, 20 and 40 acre developed black soil farms. Offices, West Palm Beach, Fla., and Kansas City, Mo.

The Community Place was the first building in the development of Security Farms Syndicate, located about 23 miles west of West Palm Beach. This postcard advertised the sale of 10-, 30-, and 40-acre "black soil farms." (Collection of Robert Carr.)

Six

CREATING NEW COMMUNITIES AND LOSING OLD ONES

Incorporated in 1925, Clewiston began as a farming and fishing village, on the northern rim of the Everglades at the southern tip of Lake Okeechobee, called Sand Point. Tampa banker A.C. Clewis came there in 1920 to found the Southern Sugar Corporation, which became U.S. Sugar in 1931. This photograph of the newly constructed main station and locomotive of the Moore Haven and Clewiston Railroad was taken on January 17, 1928. (Collection of Robert Carr.)

Hundreds of new settlers arrived in the tent city of Progresso looking for cheap farmland. The location seen in this c. 1911 real-photo postcard is now downtown Fort Lauderdale. (Collection of Robert Carr.)

The new post office and general store in Zona was built on top of the dredge pile of the South New River Canal. Zona was named after the Canal Zone by the dredge men who had dug the Panama Canal and had taken new jobs on the Everglades drainage project. Zona's name was changed to Davie in 1918. (Courtesy of the Davie Historical Society.)

The town of Everglades was created along the Barron River. George W. Storter arrived there in 1889 and in 1892 built a general store and trading post on land that would become the site of the town. (Courtesy of the State Archives of Florida.)

By the 1930s, the town of Everglades had grown to include new homes. Storter's house became the Rod and Gun Club, a popular draw for sports fishermen and hunters. (Courtesy of the Historical Museum of Southern Florida.)

Fort Lauderdale emerged as one of the principle towns for the receipt of produce transported along the New River canals from Everglades farms. The city was incorporated in 1911. (Courtesy of the Broward County Historical Commission.)

This real-photo postcard of the entrance to South Canal from Lake Okeechobee, the setting for a new hotel, was taken by Fort Lauderdale photographer Guy Phipps around 1912. (Collection of Robert Carr.)

The Ritta Hotel, originally the Bolles Hotel, as seen in this real-photo postcard, was built in 1911 by entrepreneur and raconteur Richard "Dicky" Bolles on Ritta Island off Lake Okeechobee's southeastern shore. The hotel was operated by his family. (Collection of Robert Carr.)

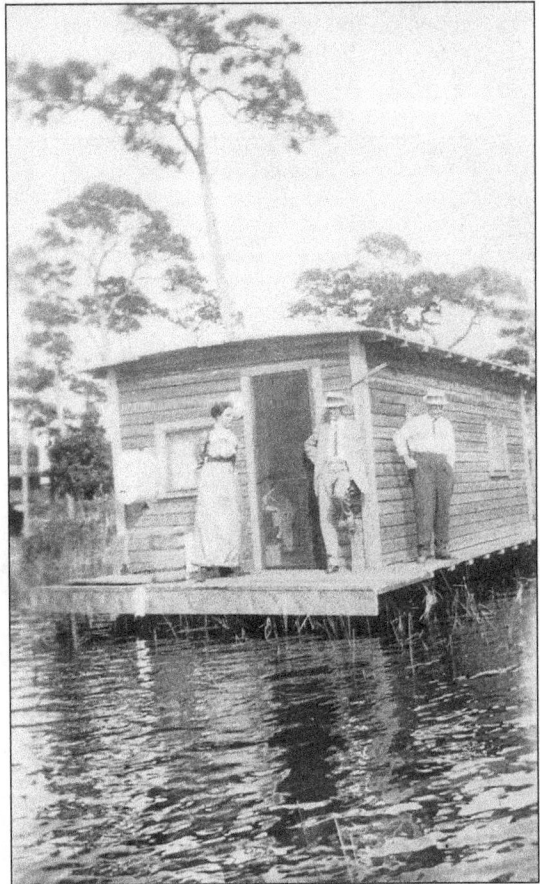

The origins of the city's reputation as the "Venice of America" can be seen in this photograph of a houseboat docked near Fort Lauderdale. The boat's occupants are unidentified. (Courtesy of Broward County Historical Commission.)

Some families and visitors traveled by houseboat to Lake Okeechobee up the New River Canal. The caption on this real-photo postcard reads, "The home of my Alligator Purse. Captured by Capt. Jack, made by his niece on this boat." Jack's houseboat is docked on Lake Okeechobee near Ritta Island around 1912. (Collection of Robert Carr.)

Canal Point was built in 1914 on the southeastern shore of Lake Okeechobee. The community was one of several that had origins in black-dirt farming. This real-photo postcard was taken around 1950. (Collection of Robert Carr.)

The coconut plantation in this c. 1912 real-photo postcard was on Cape Sable. Farming and fishing were the subsistence of settlers there. The Cape Sable community was large enough to have its own post office between 1904 and 1919. (Collection of Robert Carr.)

Viewing Cape Sable from the air around 1950 reveals the land completely cleared of buildings after the creation of the park. The park policy objective was to return the park to its natural state. (Courtesy of National Park Service, Everglades National Park, EVER 1259a.)

The Flamingo and Cape Sable settlements were the oldest communities in the area that became Everglades National Park. This photograph was taken around 1948. (Courtesy of the Historical Association of Southern Florida.)

A group of buildings in Flamingo known as the Mitchell structures included the East Coast Fisheries fish house. They were inventoried for their value as part of the park buyout. (National Park Service, Courtesy of Everglades National Park, EVER 15071a NPS 59.)

This is a photograph taken of an unidentified family standing in front of their house in Flamingo before it and other structures were bought and demolished to return the park to its natural state. (Courtesy of the Historical Museum of Southern Florida.)

Robert and an unidentified man stand in front of Robert's "mansion" at Flamingo in 1937. Flamingo residents would become a source of continual irritation for park officials, as residents continued to hunt and fish in the park. (Courtesy of Historical Museum of Southern Florida.)

Flamingo home builders were resourceful. This frame dwelling, like all those along the waterfront, stands above ground on wooden piers. The siding is palmetto thatch over tar paper. A backwoods flying buttress stabilizes the structure. Rain falling on the roof flows down dual sheet metal troughs into barrels—the community's main source of freshwater. (Courtesy of the National Park Service, Everglades National Park, EVER 12354a.)

Outhouses for waterfront properties were frequently built at the end of a dock, adding to the pollution of Florida Bay. Much of the pollution ended with the acquisition of the town by the park service that occurred soon after the hurricane of September 1948, which destroyed 18 homes in Flamingo. (Courtesy of Walter Phillips—University of Arizona: Everglades National Park, EVER17330 NPS 6.)

Displaced from Flamingo by the buyout were scores of fishermen like this unidentified man. Most fisher folk moved down to the Florida Keys or up the coast to other southwest Florida communities. (Courtesy of the Historical Museum of Southern Florida.)

This Flamingo home features shiplap siding, tar paper roof, storm shutters, flying buttresses, and a deck for hanging out the wash. (Courtesy of the National Park Service, Everglades National Park, EVER 12353a.)

Everglades and Lake Okeechobee communities were vulnerable to hurricanes because of their low elevations. Trucks are seen hauling caskets to Belle Glade after the hurricane of 1928. The storm blew west from Palm Beach across Lake Okeechobee. The lake water was pushed by the violent winds, sending a wave 15 feet high crashing through the dike on its south shore and flooding the towns of Miami Locks, South Bay, Chosen, Pahokee, and Belle Glade. Some 2,500 people died, most of them farmhands working the truck farms of the upper Glades. (Collection of Robert Carr.)

A handwritten note on the back of this scrapbook photograph reads, "Gruesome reminder of Florida hurricane September 16, 1928. This snapshot was taken in the Everglades 3 months after the storm. Dad." (Collection of Robert Carr.)

Seven

ROAD ACROSS
THE EVERGLADES

A celebratory convoy officially opens the Tamiami Trail in April 1928. (Courtesy of the Historical Museum of Southern Florida.)

The first Tamiami Trail was completed by 1901 on present-day Southwest Eighth Street in Miami. The road extended westward from Brickell Avenue to what would become the city of Coral Gables. Eventually, the Tamiami Trail would cross the Everglades and link the two coasts. (Courtesy of the Historical Museum of Southern Florida.)

Barron Collier was a wealthy businessman and publisher who, after moving to South Florida, invested millions of dollars in the construction of the Tamiami Trail and State Road 29 that connected the trail to Everglades City. He owned the Rod and Reel Club in the town of Everglades and, because of his large land holdings, became the namesake of newly formed Collier County in 1915. (Courtesy of the State Archives of Florida.)

Formerly a US Navy engineer, David Graham Copeland helped plan the Tamiami Trail. He later became chairman of the state commission to draw the boundaries of the new park. Copeland proposed, as a compromise among conflicting parties: a park area that excluded the Big Cypress Swamp, Key Largo, and Turner River—drastically shrinking the park as envisioned by Ernest Coe. The tiny town of Copeland grew out of a family farm he founded near the Big Cypress Swamp. (Courtesy of the State Archives of Florida.)

Construction of the Tamiami Trail began in 1915. The State of Florida sold 20,000 acres to J.F. Jaudon, T. Highlyman, and R.E. McDonald for $100,000. Lee, Monroe, and Dade Counties paid for the road construction, while Jaudon sold lands adjacent to the road to investors. Part of the money paid to the state was earmarked to dredge new canals to link the Tamiami Canal with outlets to existing canals. (Courtesy of the Historical Museum of Southern Florida.)

Dredge, Drill Barge & Service Boat- R.C. Hoffman Co Tamaimi Trail_ 1926-27. 30 Miles West of Miami

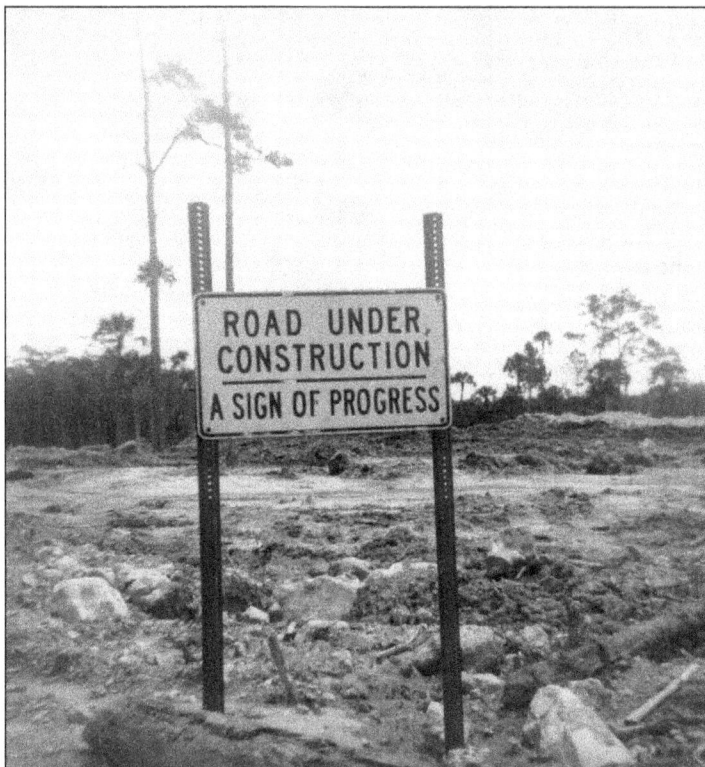

The Tamiami Trail was an ambitious project, employing hundreds of workers. It took 13 years and cost $8 million to construct. While it promised big returns for investors, it impeded the natural flow of water in the Everglades. (Courtesy of Historical Museum of Southern Florida.)

Limestone dredged from the adjacent canal was used to construct the road. The accessibility of local rock greatly reduced the cost of road construction since rock material did not have to be brought from distant quarries. (Courtesy of the Historical Museum of Southern Florida.)

The Tamiami Trail created a 108-mile link between Naples and Miami. A second, alternate road segment was constructed through Monroe County in 1921. It created a controversy, and the state ordered the road moved back to its original alignment through Collier County. The abandoned segment is present-day Loop Road. (Courtesy of Historical Museum of Southern Florida.)

A couple walks along the trail while their driver tends to the car. The Tamiami Trail offered visitors their first open view of the Everglades. (Courtesy of the Historical Museum of Southern Florida.)

This prominent gateway was constructed on the Dade-Collier County line. The arch proved to be an obstruction and eventually was demolished to allow widening of the road. (Courtesy of the Historical Museum of Southern Florida.)

The town of Everglades celebrates the road opening with a parade and ribbon-cutting. The town was jubilant with the expectation that Tamiami Trail would bring new visitors and businesses to the community. (Courtesy of the Historical Museum of Southern Florida.)

Politicians welcome Billy Bowlegs III at the opening of Tamiami Trail. Bowlegs was a prominent Seminole elder of African Seminole descent. He died at the age of 97 in 1965. (Courtesy of the Historical Museum of Southern Florida.)

Initially, the view down Tamiami Trail was a lonely vista where a car traveled miles before passing another vehicle. The road was constructed at a cost of about $25,000 per mile. (Courtesy of the Historical Museum of Southern Florida.)

The road opened the Everglades to hunters as well as through traffic. This real-photo postcard taken in the 1920s shows two deer shot by hunters on the road linking the Tamiami Trail to Everglades City. (Collection of Robert Carr.)

Seminoles and Miccosukees began camping on the spoil poles created by the dredging of the Tamiami Canal. The high and dry ground created an alternative to living on a tree island. This photograph was taken on December 27, 1927. (Collection of Robert Carr.)

The road dramatically altered Miccosukee settlement patterns, anchoring villages and camps to the highway using rocky fill pads instead of natural tree islands. (Courtesy of the National Park Service, Everglades National Park, EVER 016884.)

East-west travel routes shifted from the traditional canoe trails through the Everglades to travel along the Tamiami Canal, which ran parallel to the road. (Collection of Robert Carr.)

On the Tamiami Trail near Everglades, Collier County, Florida

The road increased visitor travel by bus. Itineraries included stops at the Miccosukee village and Ochopee. (Collection of Robert Carr.)

PAOLITA STATION, TAMIAMI TRAIL, FLORIDA
HOME OF GOOD COFFEE AND FOOD

At least six gas stations were constructed between Naples and Miami, including Paolita, located at the Collier-Dade County line. Paolita was named after Graham Copeland's wife. The postcard view dates to approximately 1930. (Collection of Robert Carr.)

The town of Ochopee was the center of tomato farming along the trail. Ochopee featured a restaurant and what was claimed to be the nation's smallest post office, as shown in this real-photo postcard from the 1950s. (Collection of Robert Carr.)

"Y'awl come eat with the Lord's" reads the sign in front of Joe & Suzzie Lord's Monroe Station, located in Collier County halfway between Miami and Naples. The building still survives west of the Miccosukee Reservation. This postcard was published in the 1960s. (Collection of Robert Carr.)

Alligator Alley was the second road constructed across the Everglades. Officially listed as State Road 84, it was built as a two-lane toll road in 1969 to link Fort Lauderdale with Naples and was known as the Everglades Parkway. In the 1990s, it was widened to four lanes and christened Alligator Alley. Built into it are culverts for water flow and safety tunnels for animal—particularly panther—crossings. (Courtesy of the Historical Museum of Southern Florida.)

Construction on a 39-square-mile Everglades jetport began in 1969 in the middle of the Big Cypress, 30 miles west of Miami. An alternative to Miami International Airport, it was touted as the jetport of the future, capable of landing supersonic jets on six-mile-long runways. The plans were scrapped after a tremendous public outcry because of the extensive environmental damage the project was causing. (Courtesy of Historical Museum of Southern Florida.)

Eight

TOURISTS, SCHOLARS, AND SCIENTISTS

Davie dairyman Hamilton C. Forman (left) and neighbor Otto Segman killed 13 diamondback rattlesnakes that had congregated on a North New River ditch bank—the only land high and dry—after the 1947 hurricane. (Courtesy of Collins Forman.)

The newly dredged Miami Canal opened up the Everglades for visitors. This real-photo postcard is captioned, "Miami Canal—Looking west dredge Miami in distance. Taken from Dam." (Collection of Robert Carr.)

In this real-photo postcard, tourists from the *Sallie* walk atop the dredge piles on the south bank of the Miami Canal. (Collection of Robert Carr.)

Visitors flocked from the Royal Palm Hotel at the mouth of the Miami River for daily trips up the river, as shown in this 1910 real-photo postcard of the *Sallie*. (Collection of Robert Carr.)

Dressed in their Sunday best, a group of tourists is boated west up the Miami Canal to view the engineering feat in this real-photo postcard from 1912. (Collection of Robert Carr.)

After the *Sallie* arrived at the headwaters of the Miami River, visitors were treated to a mule train ride. The writer notes that the cars needed new seats. The note on this 1908 real-photo postcard reads, "Everglades R.R.," while the sign on the train simply states, "EVG RR." (Collection of Robert Carr.)

This cart was pulled along a narrow-gauge railroad through a lush tropical hammock. This postcard view is titled, "A Short R.R. in the Everglades, near Miami, Fla." (Collection of Robert Carr.)

Miami, Florida, In the Everglades, Observatory Tower.

The observation tower was located at the headwaters of the north fork of the Miami River near present-day Southwest Twenty-ninth Avenue in urban Miami. (Collection of Robert Carr.)

The Observatory in Everglades, Miami, Fla.

Tourists climbed about 40 feet up to the top of the observation tower to view the Everglades a few hundred feet to the west. After the dredging of the Miami River, boat trips to the observation tower were abandoned because of new access to the Glades through the Miami Canal. (Collection of Robert Carr.)

Curiosity about the Everglades attracted an increasing number of scientists who began cataloging its plants and animals. Charles Torrey Simpson, a botanist, conservationist, and longtime resident of Miami, authored numerous books on the area. Here, Simpson (left) and companions carry cut strands of palm. (Courtesy of the Historical Museum of Southern Florida.)

Simpson had worked at the Smithsonian Institution in 1889, as well as the National Museum of Natural History from 1883 to 1902. He estimated that his backyard tropical hammock in Lemon City had been visited by over 50,000 people. He was a strong advocate of creating a national park in the Everglades. (Courtesy of the State Archives of Florida.)

John Kunkel Small (right) was a botanist and the first curator of museums at the New York Botanical Garden. His first trip to Florida was in 1901, and he traveled deep into the Everglades with his wife, Elizabeth, and four children. He published over 450 articles that culminated with his 1929 book *From Eden to Sahara: Florida's Tragedy*, describing the destruction of south Florida's environment. (Courtesy of the State Archives of Florida.)

John Kunkel Small braved long trips deep into the sawgrass. In this scene, photographed on the edge of Royal Palm Hammock on July 29, 1915, his sons John and George help dig the truck out of a hole. (Collection of Robert Carr.)

One of Small's sons stands beside an isolated specimen of bald cypress (*Taxodium distichum*) in March 1911 between Camp Jackson and Royal Palm Hammock in the Everglades. Small urged that this ecological El Dorado, where subtropical and temperate regions met and mingled, should be preserved. (Collection of Robert Carr.)

John Gifford, a forester at the University of Miami, introduced melaleuca (*Melaleuca quinquenervia*) into the Everglades to facilitate drainage. He had no idea how detrimental the Australian plant would be, as it choked out all the native species, absorbed groundwater, and formed monoforest "deserts" across the Glades. Millions of dollars have been spent removing this noxious plant. (Courtesy of the Historical Museum of Southern Florida.)

Charles Brookfield, a naturalist and adventurer, cuts through the brush on Cape Sable. Brookfield moved to Miami from Philadelphia at age 21. He worked for the US Coast and Geodetic Survey mapping Florida Bay from 1934 to 1936. After the end of World War II and hunting German U-boats for the Coast Guard, seeing action in Sicily and North Africa and joining the invasion of Normandy, Brookfield returned to Florida. (Courtesy of the Historical Museum of Southern Florida.)

Brookfield was hired in 1946 as an Audubon warden to protect the Shark River rookeries before they became part of Everglades National Park. This portrait was taken in Cape Sable between 1946 and 1948. In 1949, he coauthored *They All Called it Tropical*, a popular book on Everglades and Keys history. (Courtesy of the National Park Service, Everglades National Park, EVER 12843 NPS 134.)

Everglades tree snails (*Liguus fasciatus*) were studied by Charles Torrey Simpson, who collected them at Long Pine Key. Other conchologists, scholars, and collectors interested in the snails were Dr. Henry Augustus Pilsbry, Dr. William J. Clench of Harvard University, Dr. Frank Craighead, Archie Jones, and Charles Mosier, former superintendent of Royal Palm Park. (Courtesy of the State Archives of Florida.)

From 1934 to 1935, the Smithsonian Institution directed the first systematic investigations of archaeological sites in the Everglades, although all of this work was conducted outside the park boundaries. The project used scores of laborers paid by the Works Progress Administration (WPA) under the supervision of surveyor Karl Squires. State archaeologist Vernon Lame directed the work, and he was soon succeeded by state geologist Alfred Coe. (Collection of Robert Carr.)

Matt Sterling of the Smithsonian Institution uncovers a prehistoric horse conch anchor from an Everglades tree island as part of the 1934–1935 WPA archaeology project. (Collection of Robert Carr.)

John Goggin was the first archaeologist to create an inventory of prehistoric sites in the Everglades. He grew up in Miami and visited the Flagami site in 1931. In the 1940s, he conducted numerous archaeological surveys and investigations of tree islands. In this rare photograph of Goggin (right), taken around 1950, his swamp buggy is stuck in the muck. (Collection of Robert Carr.)

Ales Hrdlicka, born in 1869, was an anthropologist from the US National Museum, now the Smithsonian Institution. He documented numerous sites in the southern Everglades along Florida Bay and became a major advocate of the creation of Everglades National Park. Hrdlicka stated that the Turner River site was so important to science that it should be preserved for posterity. (Courtesy of the Library of Congress.)

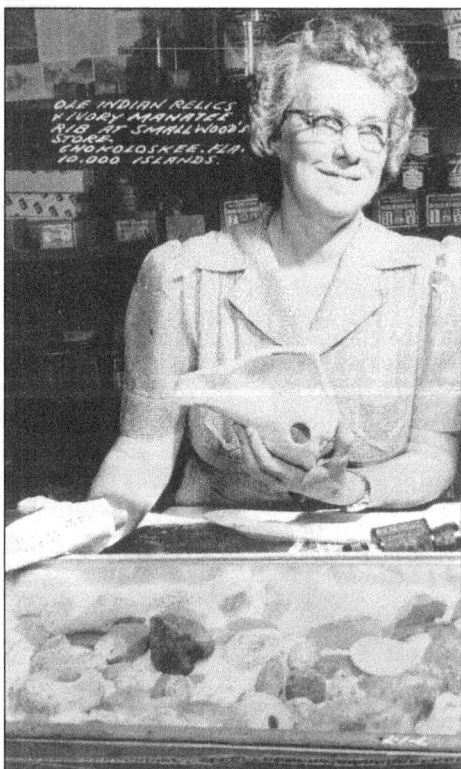

Thelma Smallwood operated Smallwood's Store at Chokoloskee, where local prehistoric artifacts were on exhibit. The Smallwood family owned 167 acres. Thelma reminded archaeologist Ales Hrdlicka in 1936 of the importance of Chokoloskee and the Turner River archaeological sites as part of the proposed Everglades National Park, urging him to persuade park officials to pay a good fair price for her land. (Collection of Robert Carr.)

George L. Espenlaub ran tours of the Everglades. His swamp buggy balloon tires helped him navigate the muck and mud. These photographs were taken in 1954. (Both, courtesy of the State Archives of Florida.)

Wind Across the Everglade, released in 1958, was the first film to fuel popular interest in Everglades history. In the photograph are Burl Ives (left), who plays Cottonmouth, hermit Roy Ozmer (center), and actor/boxer Tony Gelanto (right). (Courtesy of the State Archives of Florida.)

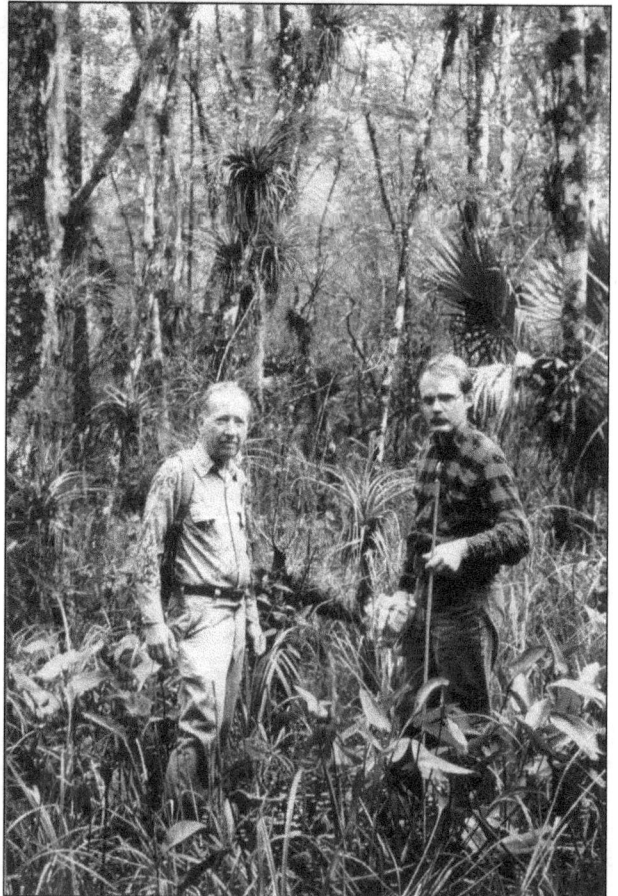

Carlyle A. Luer, MD (left) stands with Stig Dalström, a Swedish botanical illustrator, in the Fakahatchee Strand in March 1988. Dr. Luer, a surgeon, orchid scientist, and advocate of the preservation of natural areas, has discovered and described thousands of new orchids and authored numerous articles and books. He was instrumental in founding Marie Selby Botanical Gardens in Sarasota. (Courtesy of Dr. Carlyle A. Luer.)

Nine

CREATING A
TROPICAL PARK

Daniel Beard was a National Park Service biologist whose pre-park survey of Everglades wildlife showed several species to be on the verge of extinction. In 1947, he became the park's first superintendent. (Courtesy of the National Park Service, Everglades National Park, EVER 17940.)

Jungle and Palm in Womans State Park, near Homestead, Fla.

Pictured in this c. 1915 postcard, Paradise Key was known to botanists as early as the 1880s. Its large strand of royal palms set it apart from any other botanical community in the United States. (Collection of Robert Carr.)

In 1910, J.E. Ingraham, surveyor for the Florida East Coast Railroad, told Mrs. Kirk Munroe, president of the Florida Federation of Women's Clubs, about Paradise Key and its royal palms. She asked that the land be donated to her organization to create a park. (Courtesy of the National Park Service, Everglades National Park, NP 5128.)

102

May Mann Jennings, the wife of Florida governor William Sherman Jennings, was president of the Florida Federation of Women's Clubs from 1914 to 1917 and used her considerable social charm and political skills to lobby her husband and other state politicians to create Woman's State Park, which was renamed Royal Palm Park. (Courtesy of the State Archives of Florida.)

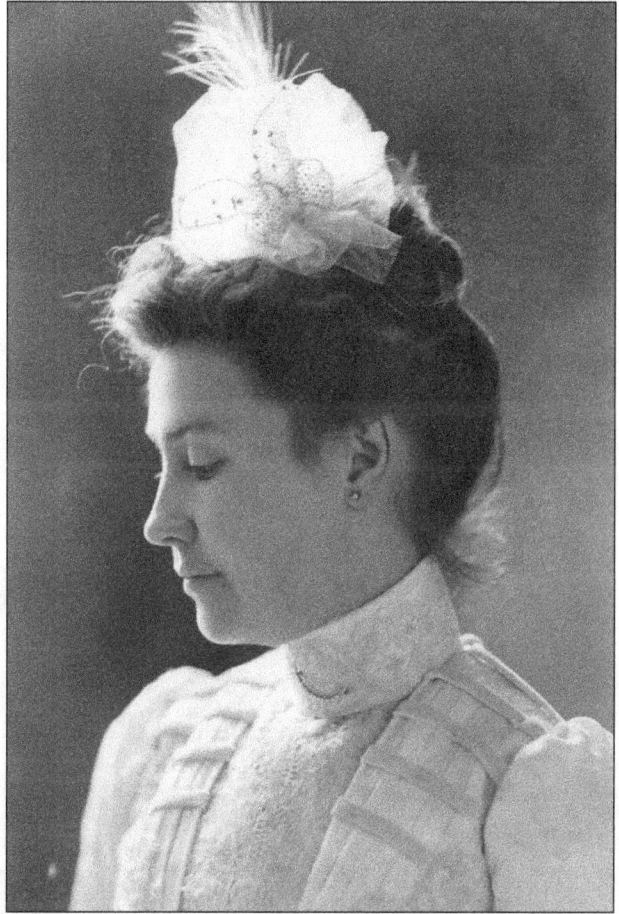

The first road through the Everglades followed the alignment of the Krome survey into Royal Palm Hammock. The road was cut in 1915 by the Model Land Company. (Courtesy of the Historical Museum of Southern Florida.)

The road was named the Ingraham Highway in honor of J.E. Ingraham's contribution towards creating the park. The dedication of Royal Palm State Park occurred on November 22, 1916. More than 50 automobiles carrying a total of 750 people arrived for the occasion. (Courtesy of the National Park Service, Everglades National Park, EVER 15179.)

The Royal Palm Lodge was completed in 1919. Charles A. Mosier was the park's first curator. Lodge revenues were in the red; fires and the 1926 hurricane required substantial financial aid from the state to keep it operating. (Courtesy of Historical Museum of Southern Florida.)

In 1934, Royal Palm Park was declared a conservation area eligible for federal aid. The Civilian Conservation Corps (CCC) was assigned to the park from November 1934 through June 1935. (Courtesy of the Broward County Historical Commission.)

In 1929, the Federation of Women's Clubs offered Paradise Key to the federal government to become the heart of Everglades National Park. The donation of Royal Palm State Park was commemorated with a bronze plaque on October 10, 1947. (Courtesy of the National Park Service, Everglades National Park, EVER 30745 NPS 127.)

Ernst Coe was the spark plug in the movement to create an Everglades National Park. Coe was a landscape architect who arrived in Miami in 1925. It was an ornithologist, Harold H. Bailey, who first suggested that a park was needed to protect the Everglades's dwindling bird population. Coe founded the Tropical Everglades Park Association in 1928 to spearhead the effort. (Courtesy of the National Park Service, Everglades National Park, EVER 22816.)

Coe promoted the need for a national park with constant lobbying of political officials. He even printed postcards with a powerful endorsement from conservationist Gifford Pinchot: "It is a land of strangeness separate and apart from the common things we know so well. . . . There are more fish around Cape Sable than I ever saw anywhere else in a lifetime of fishing." (Collection of Robert Carr.)

GOVERNOR'S OFFICE
HARRISBURG, PA,
April 30, 1931.

Dear Mr. Coe:

". . . It is as interesting in its way as, for example, Glacier National Park is in its very different way . . . It is a land of strangeness separate and apart from the common things we know so well. . . . A new world to play in, a good place to be in summer as well as winter. There are more fish around Cape Sable than I ever saw anywhere else in a lifetime of fishing."

Sincerely yours,

GIFFORD PINCHOT

Issued by
The Tropic Everglades
National Park Associ-
ation, County Court
House, Miami, Fla.

At Coe's instigation, the federal government formed a special committee of the National Parks Association to study the feasibility of a national park in the Everglades. In February 1930, Coe arranged for the committee to inspect the proposed park by car and by Goodyear blimp, after which he led them across the Everglades for three days on a boat. Those on the blimp tour included Dr. David Fairchild, Ernest Coe (far right), Congresswoman Ruth Bryan Owen (center), and Horace M. Albright, director of the National Park Service. The committee's favorable report helped build a groundswell of support for the park. (Courtesy of the Historical Museum of Southern Florida.)

The boundaries of the park were a constant source of debate, with Coe favoring the largest possible area to include much of the Big Cypress Swamp and Key Largo. The initial acquisition plan left out Chokoloskee, Key Largo, and the Hole-in-the-Donut, a parcel used for farming. (Courtesy of City of Miami News Bureau: Everglades National Park, EVER 15217.)

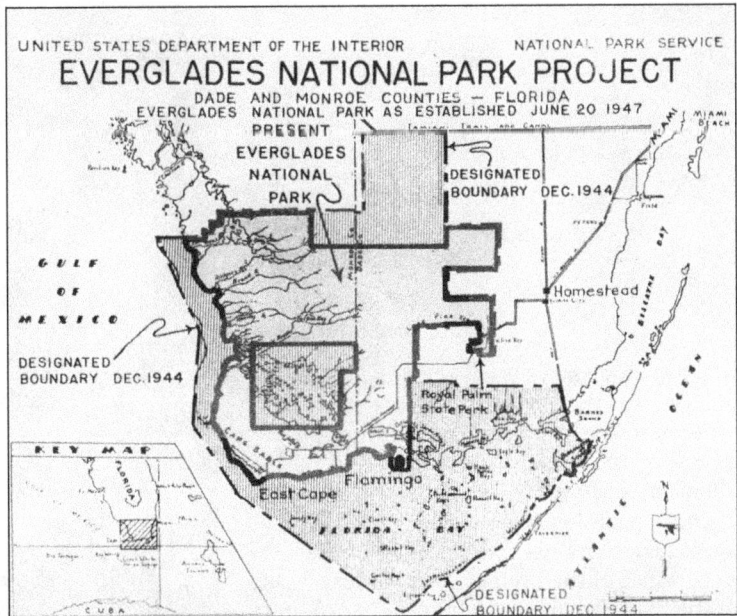

Marjory Stoneman Douglas was born in April 1890. Her talent and a lifetime of success as a journalist, author, and environmentalist underscored her passion for the Everglades. Her father, Frank Stoneman, editor of the predecessor of the *Miami Herald*, opposed Napoleon Bonaparte Broward's plan to drain the Everglades. Douglas's voice as a well-established *Miami Herald* columnist gave her a wide audience. (Courtesy of the Historical Museum of Southern Florida.)

Marjory Stoneman Douglas convinced publishers of the Rivers of America series to scrap their idea of her writing a book on the Miami River and instead allow her to write *The Everglades: River of Grass*, published in 1947. Her book awakened a national consciousness of the importance of the Everglades. (Courtesy of the State Archives of Florida.)

The 1.3 million–acre Everglades National Park was formally dedicated on December 6, 1947, by Pres. Harry S. Truman at a ceremony in Everglades City. (Courtesy of the Historical Museum of Southern Florida.)

President Truman is seen receiving a patchwork jacket from Seminole chief William McKinnley Osceola at the park dedication ceremony on December 6, 1947. The establishment of the park would offer new opportunities and challenges for the Seminoles and eventually lead to the creation of the Miccosuki Reservation along the Tamiami Trail. (Courtesy of the National Park Service, Everglades National Park, EVER 17728a NPS 7.)

The festivities inspired the baking of a large cake in the shape of Florida as hundreds of visitors arrived in Everglades City, the new park's western gateway, for the dedication. (Courtesy of the Historical Museum of Southern Florida.)

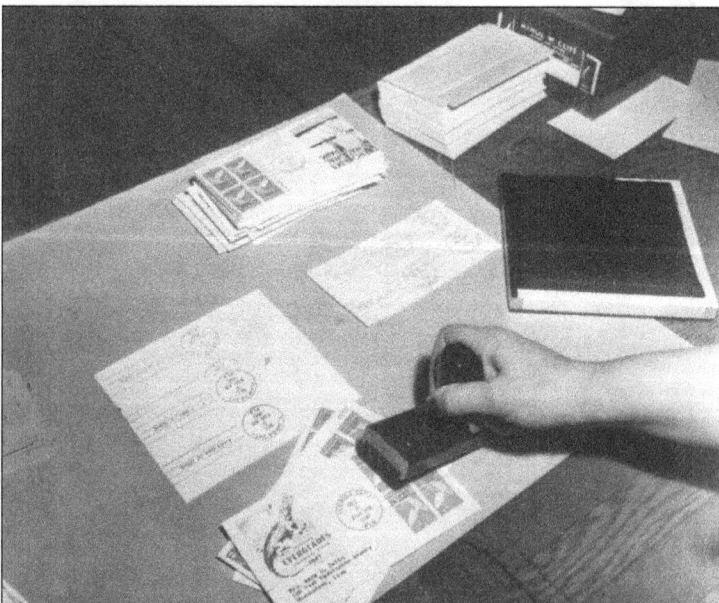

A first-day cover was issued commemorating the park with a specially designed 3¢ stamp. The special stamp was postmarked at the Flamingo Post Office. Overall, 800,000 stamps were sold, generating $34,000 in revenue. (Courtesy of the Historical Museum of Southern Florida.)

Ten

INTERPRETING THE PARK

Rangers survey the park
from a swamp buggy, the
most effective vehicle
for making patrols. In
November 1949, a total of
2,028 miles of parkland
were patrolled: 537
miles by roadway and
1,491 by water routes.
(Courtesy of the State
Archives of Florida.)

Rangers set signs to mark the new park's boundaries. A budget of $87,000 was provided for the park's first year of operation in 1948. (Courtesy of the Historical Museum of Southern Florida.)

The swamp buggy was one of the principal ways for scientists and rangers to move across the park. (Courtesy of the National Park Service, Everglades National Park, EVER 15214.)

Alexander Graham Bell is said to have invented the airboat in 1905 in Canada as a platform for testing engines and propellers. An associate of his, Glenn Curtiss, registered the first airboat in Florida—the Curtiss "Scooter"—in 1920. Airboats became indispensable in the Glades. In this photograph, a Miccosukee tinkers with his airboat motor. (Courtesy of the Historical Museum of Southern Florida.)

Airboats provide rapid deployment and transportation for patrolling the glades. Rescuing deer from rising waters is an important task for rangers during periods of flooding from heavy rains and hurricanes. (Courtesy of the Historical Museum of Southern Florida.)

Accessing the park by roads meant building bridges to maintain adequate water flow. The creation of a road and bridge infrastructure was an important part of opening the park to the public. (Courtesy of the National Park Service, Everglades National Park EVER 012982.)

Patterns of precious freshwater flow were also maintained by culverts buried below the road. In winter months, water tables fell so low that water only flowed through the sloughs and canals. (Courtesy of the National Park Service, Everglades National Park, EVER 012980.)

The construction of park roads had to be carefully planned and cautiously implemented to minimize collateral damage to natural and archaeological features. When the park opened, no roads existed except for the Ingraham Highway, which was not under park-service control. (Courtesy of the National Park Service, Everglades National Park, EVER 012983.)

The first visitor entrance was located at Long Key. Its simple chickee form was in keeping with Seminole and Miccosukee tradition. (Courtesy of the State Archives of Florida.)

The park ranger station at Flamingo was constructed in the 1950s. Rangers used the Flamingo and Coot Bay stations to patrol over 800 square miles of coastal waters. (Courtesy of the National Park Service, Everglades National Park, EVER 012237.)

Tourists examine fishing boats docked at Coot Bay in this c. 1950 photograph. In January 1949, park superintendent Dan Beard reported that no restrooms existed in the park except for a latrine over the canal at Coot Bay. (Courtesy of the Historical Museum of Southern Florida.)

The Mahogany Hammock boardwalk allowed visitors to experience crossing the sawgrass prairie into a hammock. Mahogany hammock was "discovered" by ranger Edwin Stephanic in April 1948. The largest tree was 10 feet, two inches in diameter. (Courtesy of the State Archives of Florida.)

The Anhinga Trail (formerly known as the Taylor Slough Trail) boardwalk extended from Royal Palm Visitor Center into the adjacent slough. The first boardwalk was opened in December 1949. (Courtesy of the State Archives of Florida.)

The Shark Valley tower construction involved building a wide, gradually sloping ramp for wheelchair access. Construction began in 1964. (Courtesy of the National Park Service, Everglades National Park, EVER 27Le_1964.)

Here, the observation platform, at a height of 65 feet, is in the last phase of construction. It opened to visitors in 1965. (Courtesy of the National Park Service, Everglades National Park, EVER 271_d_1964.)

When the interpretive tower was completed, it provided a spectacular panoramic view of Shark Valley. A 15-mile tram road, where motor vehicles are prohibited, brings visitors to the tower. (Courtesy of the National Park Service, Everglades National Park, EVER 12715.)

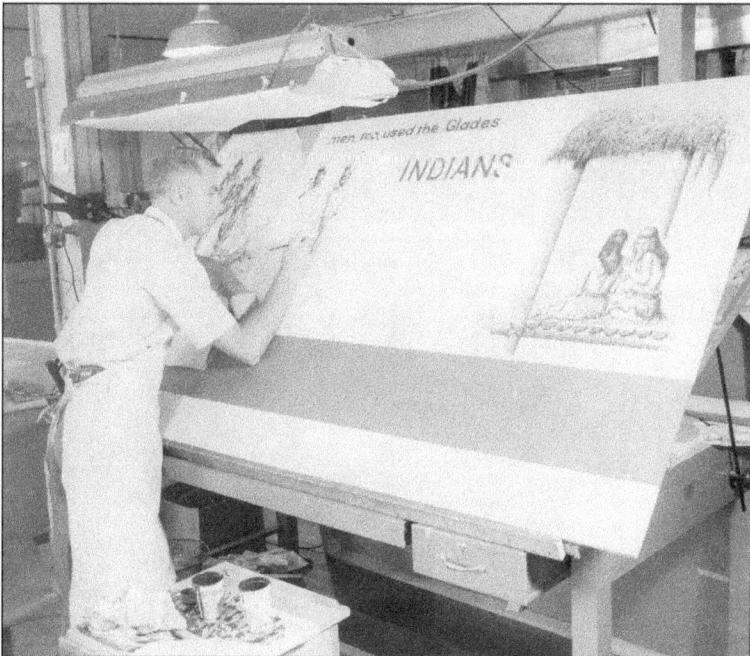

The first park exhibits were designed and built for the Anhinga Interpretive Center. Expert artists collaborated with scientists to create, by hand, graphic interpretations of the park's ecology and history. (Courtesy of the National Park Service, Everglades National Park, EVER 12650.)

The Royal Palm Interpretive Center displayed some of the park's first exhibits. Thirsty visitors could purchase an ice-cold Pepsi for 10¢ a bottle. (Courtesy of the National Park Service, Everglades National Park, EVER 012075.)

By April 1949, over 10,000 people had visited Royal Palm Hammock. The Royal Palm Visitor Center shown in this real-photo postcard was built in 1952, replacing the original Royal Palm Lodge, which was moved to Homestead. (Collection of Robert Carr.)

This photograph shows the new eastern entrance to Everglades National Park around 1958. By that year, the park had increased in size to 1,400,500 acres from 460,000 acres in 1947. (Courtesy of the National Park Service, Everglades National Park, EVER 015520.)

A ranger monitors conditions in the park. In the park's early history, confrontations between rangers and alligator poachers were commonplace. (Courtesy of the State Archives of Florida.)

A park ranger interprets the natural features of Shark Valley to a group of children. The opening of the Shark Valley Tram allowed visitors the first public access to the heart of the Everglades. (Courtesy of the Historical Museum of Southern Florida.)

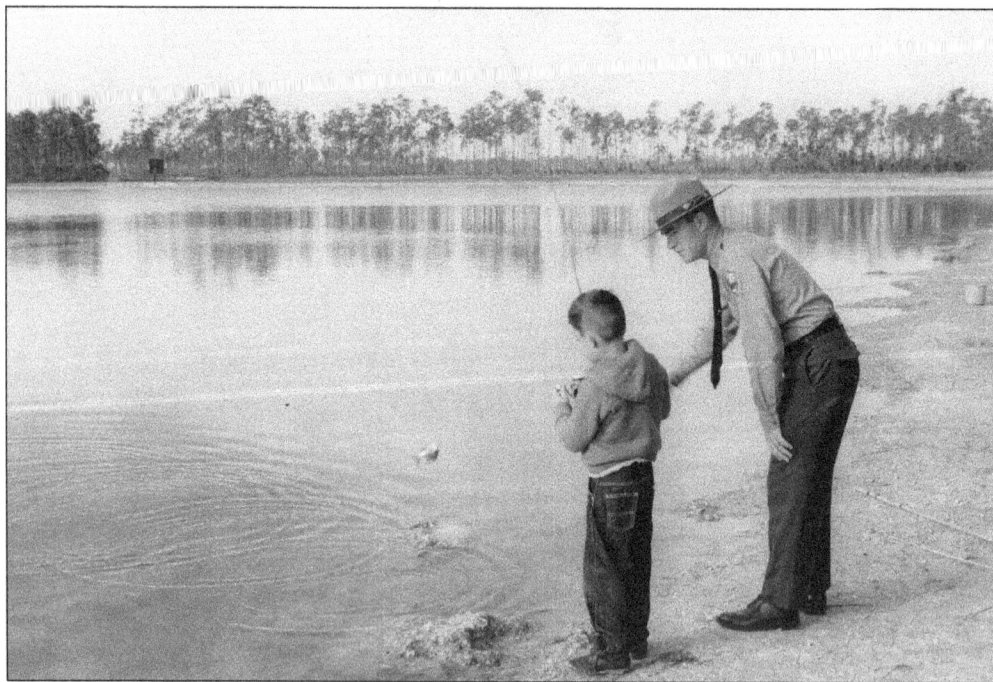

The opening of the park provided visitors opportunities for fishing. A park ranger shows a boy how to land a fish. When the park opened, fishing was prohibited in the Taylor Slough, where birds congregated. (Courtesy of the National Park Service, Everglades National Park, EVER 017458.)

A park ranger guides a tour of the mangrove coastline at the southern end of the park. The Florida Bay coast offers numerous estuaries for canoeing and boating. (Courtesy of the Historical Museum of Southern Florida.)

Scientists gather data from gauges measuring fluctuations in water level. Unusually low water tables could result in increased risk of fires and decreases in animal population. (Courtesy of the National Park Service, Everglades National Park, EVER 012987.)

The Cuban missile crisis created unforeseen pressures on the park. In October 1962, missile batteries were installed in the Hole-in-the-Donut to discourage a possible attack on the United States by Soviet and Cuban forces. (Courtesy of the Historical Museum of Southern Florida.)

A member of the Tactical Air Command manning the Nike missile base lights up. One hundred and forty military personnel were stationed at the base. Civilian access to the area was severely restricted for the duration of the crisis. (Courtesy of the Historical Museum of Southern Florida.)

After drainage, fires became more common in the Everglades, in some instances spreading into tree-island hammocks that, because of their higher moisture content, had formerly been resistant to fire. In January 1948, four fires were reported in the park. (Courtesy of the National Park Service, Everglades National Park, EVER 17029.)

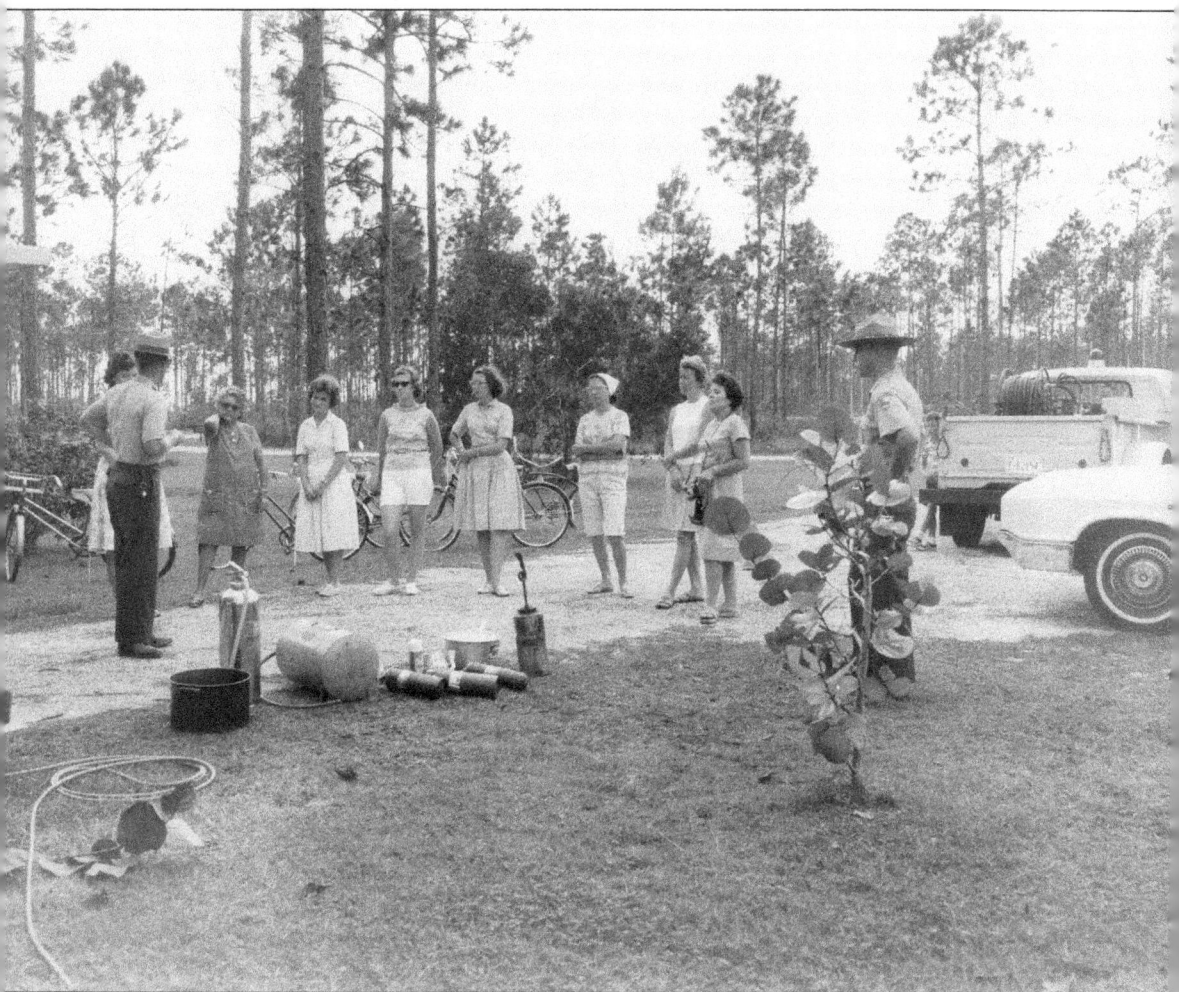

Ranger Zeb McKinney gives a group of volunteers a safety demonstration during Fire Prevention Week. Fire control has been an important part of park operations since its inception. Larger fires caused by the decrease in water levels destroyed bird rookeries and hardwood hammocks that previous to drainage would have been resistant to fires. (Courtesy of the National Park Service, Everglades National Park, NPS 140.)

Visit us at
arcadiapublishing.com

www.ingramcontent.com/pod-product-compliance
Lightning Source LLC
Chambersburg PA
CBHW080629110426
42813CB00006B/1637